At the TOP of the WORLD

By Cindy Trumbore

Modern Curriculum Press

Modern Curriculum Press

An Imprint of Pearson Learning
299 Jefferson Road, P.O. Box 480
Parsippany, NJ 07054–0480

http://www.mcschool.com

Credits

All photographs ©Pearson Learning unless otherwise noted.

Photos: Cover: Jeff Schultz/Alaska Stock Images. 1: Donnezan/Explorer/Photo
Researchers, Inc. 5: E.R. Degginger/Animals Animals. 6: Wolfgang Kaehler. 7:
Bryan & Cherry Alexander. 8: Michael Lewis/Corbis-Bettman. 9: Ken Graham/Ken
Graham Agency. 10: Trombleys Images/ Ken Graham Agency. 11: Galen
Rowell/Corbis-Bettman. 12: Bryan & Cherry Alexander. 14: Bryan & Cherry
Alexander/Photo Researchers, Inc. 15: Bill Bacon/ Ken Graham Agency. 16: Bryan &
Cherry Alexander. 17: Chris Arend/Alaska Stock.com. 18 & 19: Tiziana & Gianni
Baldizzone/Corbis-Bettman. 20: Lowell Georgia/Corbis-Bettman. 21: Bryan &
Cherry Alexander. 22: Tapio Korjus/East Side, Inc. 23: Pat O'Hara/Corbis-Bettman.
24: Lawrence Migdale/Tony Stone Images. 25: David E. Myers/Tony Stone Images.
26: m.l Johnny Johnson/Alaska Stock.com. 26: b.r. Jim Zipp/Photo Researchers, Inc.
27: Michael Durham/ENP Images. 28: Gerry Ellis/ ENP Images. 29: Bryan & Cherry
Alexander. 30: Charles Kreb/Tony Stone Images. 31: Laurie Campbell/Tony Stone
Images

Cover and book design by Lisa Ann Arcuri

ISBN: 0-7652-1378-8

1 2 3 4 5 6 7 8 9 10 LB 08 07 06 05 04 03 02 01 00 99

Contents

For Dad, who always gave me
a ride when it was cold out

Chapter 1
The Arctic

Think about a land where it is cold and dark for most of the year. In the summer the sun never sets. This place is called the Arctic. It is at the top of the world.

The Arctic is a land of snow, ice, and polar bears.

During the Arctic summer the sun shines all the time, even at night. For this reason the Arctic is sometimes called the Land of the Midnight Sun.

Summer lasts only two months from the end of June to the end of August. Then winter comes. The sun is always low in the sky. It is dark most of the time. Everything freezes and stays frozen for ten months.

A winter day in the Arctic

Can you find the eider duck sitting on the tundra?

In the Arctic the land is too cold and dry for tall trees to grow. Some plants do live there. They are small like grasses and bushes.

Many kinds of animals live there. Some large animals are polar bears, seals, and walruses. Small animals like birds and foxes live there, too.

An Arctic village

People live in the Arctic. What do you think it would be like to live at the top of the world? The best way to find out is to see what life is like for some of the Arctic people.

Meet Vivi Mala. She lives in the Arctic. Vivi and her family know the best ways to live in such a cold and frozen world.

Vivi Mala

Cold*Fact

A group of people who live in the Arctic are the Inuit (IHN oo iht). Their name means "the people."

Chapter 2
Old and New Ways

Vivi and her family live a life that is both new and old. The new ways make life easier. The old ways help Vivi's family remember how their people learned to live in the Arctic.

Woman fishing

Inuits hunt in a boat called an umiak.

If Vivi had lived in the Arctic long ago, her family would have hunted and fished for food. They would have searched for seals and walruses. They would have also hunted whales and wild deer called caribou.

The Saami people still herd reindeer today.

Some Arctic people who lived long ago were reindeer herders. The reindeer moved from place to place to look for food. The herders followed the reindeer.

In the past the people got everything they needed from animals. They ate meat and fish. They made oil from animal fat to light their lamps. They used animal bones for tools.

The people sewed animal skins together to make clothing. Most clothes were jackets with hoods and suits lined with fur. Shoes were also made from animal skins.

A Nenet mother wraps her baby in fur.

People travel on sleds pulled by reindeer.

Some Arctic people used dogsleds to travel and hunt. Teams of dogs pulled the sleds over the snow. People who herded reindeer used those animals to pull their sleds.

Most Arctic villages long ago were on the shores of the ocean and along rivers. In spring and summer the water was not frozen. Then families could fish with nets and sharp tools.

The people could also travel in boats. The Inuits used boats called kayaks for seal hunts. These small boats held just one or two people.

A kayak is a small boat.

An Inuit finishes a snow igloo.

Arctic people used to build houses
out of things they found around them.
Some people lived in tents made of animal
skins. Others made houses of stone or
hard-packed dirt.

Some Inuits used a special house for
winter hunting. It was called a snow igloo.
The people cut blocks of snow. They
placed the blocks on top of each other. The
igloo kept out the wind and cold.

16

Arctic people still hunt and fish even though there are new ways of life. Many of them do these things only on the weekends, or when they camp in the summer. They might work in an office or a factory during the week.

Inuit children fish through the ice.

Today most Arctic people like Vivi live in modern homes with electric lights. They watch TV and have telephones. They travel on snowmobiles instead of dogsleds. Yet the people don't want to forget the old ways even though life has changed.

Even dogs ride on snowmobiles today.

Cold*Fact

The word "igloo" means any kind of home to the Inuit people. Only a few of the Inuits made snow igloos.

Chapter 3
Crafts and Games

The old ways are still important to Vivi's people in other ways. When they have time, many Arctic people like to make beautiful crafts. Some people still make baskets and clothing today in the same way their people have done for many years.

The Saami weave cloth on a loom.

A figure carved from soapstone

Carving is another craft from long ago. The people use a piece of stone or bone. They cut away pieces of the bone to make the shape of an animal or person.

There are new and old ways for Vivi to have fun. Sports and games are popular. Many towns have gyms where children love to play basketball in the winter. The children also play old games that Arctic people have played for a long time.

High kick is played with a leather ball.

In some parts of Alaska, children like to tell stories with their "story knives." They use the knives to draw a house in the mud or snow. Then they use the picture to tell a story about the people who live there.

Some Arctic people still sing in an old way called yoiking. This means singing like the thing you are singing about. If someone is singing about a bear, he or she would use a growly voice.

Yoik singer Wimme Saari

Drum dancing

Many people also enjoy drum dancing. A drum dance acts out the old ways of their villages. The dancers might pretend to be hunting or picking berries. They might move their hands to show they are fishing.

Another old game is the Blanket Toss. Hunters were bounced high in blankets held by their friends. The hunters looked for animals across the flat land. Today the toss is just for fun.

People playing Blanket Toss

Cold*Fact

Many Arctic people like the same winter sports that other people do. They enjoy skating and skiing.

Chapter 4
The Tundra

The cold, treeless land where Vivi and her family live is called the tundra. She shares this land with many different kinds of animals and birds. She may see a polar bear or a grizzly bear. Grizzly bears eat berries and small animals. Polar bears hunt for seals out on the ice.

A mother polar bear with her cubs

Some of the animals that Vivi sees on the tundra change color in the winter. The Arctic hare and the Arctic fox have dark fur in summer. Their fur turns white as snow at the end of the summer. The thick white fur helps hide the animals. They can't be seen on the snowy winter tundra.

Fox in winter coat

Hare in summer coat

Lemming

Lemmings dig under the snow in winter. Other animals like the reindeer move to forests near the tundra when winter comes.

Finally the snow melts in the spring. The tundra blooms with plants and berries that are good to eat. Then the animals return.

Arctic snowy owl

A few birds, like the snowy owl, live on the tundra year round. Other birds live there only in the summer. Some summer birds are big, like swans and geese. Some are small, like sparrows.

Many insects live on the tundra. More mosquitoes live there than any other place on Earth. Butterflies and bumblebees live there, too.

Some big animals Vivi might see are seals and walruses. Seals swim under the ice to find food. They come up on land to rest. Their babies stay on land until they learn to swim.

A young ringed seal

Walruses lying on rocks

Walruses also live in the water and on the shores. They find their food in the water. They come on shore to raise their babies.

Big whales live in the icy Arctic waters. Some Arctic people still hunt for whales. The whales are hard to find and catch.

Today the land where Vivi lives is changing. Animals have less space in places where people work to remove oil and coal from the land. Vivi and her people need help to keep the Arctic beautiful. They want to find ways for animals and people to share the land.

Arctic tern

Cold*Fact

A bird called the Arctic tern lives on the tundra in the summer. Then it flies all the way to the bottom of the world for the winter.

Glossary

Arctic [AHRK tihk] the land and water at the top part of the world

carving [KAHRV ing] cutting away at wood or stone to make a figure

crafts [krafts] things made with special skill by hand

dogsled [DAWG sled] a sled pulled by a team of dogs

herders [HURD urz] people who follow and direct any group of animals

igloo [IHG loo] a snow igloo is a house made of blocks of snow

kayak [KYE ak] a small boat that holds one or two people

tundra [TUN druh] a treeless, frozen, flat land in the far north